Dear Parents:

MW01125527

Congratulations! Your child is taki.
the first steps on an exciting journey.
The destination? Independent reading!

STEP INTO READING® will help your child get there. The program offers five steps to reading success. Each step includes fun stories and colorful art or photographs. In addition to original fiction and books with favorite characters, there are Step into Reading Non-Fiction Readers, Phonics Readers and Boxed Sets, Sticker Readers, and Comic Readers—a complete literacy program with something to interest every child.

Learning to Read, Step by Step!

Ready to Read   Preschool–Kindergarten
• big type and easy words • rhyme and rhythm • picture clues
For children who know the alphabet and are eager to begin reading.

Reading with Help   Preschool–Grade 1
• basic vocabulary • short sentences • simple stories
For children who recognize familiar words and sound out new words with help.

Reading on Your Own   Grades 1–3
• engaging characters • easy-to-follow plots • popular topics
For children who are ready to read on their own.

Reading Paragraphs   Grades 2–3
• challenging vocabulary • short paragraphs • exciting stories
For newly independent readers who read simple sentences with confidence.

Ready for Chapters   Grades 2–4
• chapters • longer paragraphs • full-color art
For children who want to take the plunge into chapter books but still like colorful pictures.

STEP INTO READING® is designed to give every child a successful reading experience. The grade levels are only guides; children will progress through the steps at their own speed, developing confidence in their reading. The F&P Text Level on the back cover serves as another tool to help you choose the right book for your child.

Remember, a lifetime love of reading starts with a single step!

To my father —Z.A.

*To my daughter and our endless
fun at the pool, bike riding in
the park, and me winning every
badminton game. Sorry. —F.W.*

Text copyright © 2025 by Zaila Avant-garde
Cover art and interior illustrations copyright © 2025 by Felicia Whaley

All rights reserved. Published in the United States by Random House Children's Books,
a division of Penguin Random House LLC, 1745 Broadway, New York, NY 10019.

Step into Reading, Random House, and the Random House colophon are registered trademarks
of Penguin Random House LLC.

Visit us on the Web!
StepIntoReading.com
rhcbooks.com

Educators and librarians, for a variety of teaching tools, visit us at RHTeachersLibrarians.com

Library of Congress Cataloging-in-Publication Data
Names: Avant-garde, Zaila, author. | Whaley, Felicia, illustrator.
Title: Sports are fun! / by Zaila Avant-garde ; illustrated by Felicia Whaley.
Description: New York : Random House Children's Books, [2025] | Series: Step into reading |
Audience: Ages 3–7 | Summary: "A step 1 leveled reader about the joy of playing sports, by
basketball star Zaila Avant-garde" —Provided by publisher.
Identifiers: LCCN 2024031242 (print) | LCCN 2024031243 (ebook) |
ISBN 978-0-593-57170-5 (paperback) | ISBN 978-0-593-57171-2 (lib. bdg.) |
ISBN 978-0-593-57172-9 (ebook)
Subjects: LCSH: Sports—Juvenile literature.
Classification: LCC GV705.4 .A93 2025 (print) | LCC GV705.4 (ebook) |
DDC 796—dc23/eng/20240706

Printed in the United States of America
10 9 8 7 6 5 4 3 2 1
First Edition

This book has been officially leveled by using the F&P Text Level Gradient™ Leveling System.

Random House Children's Books supports the First Amendment and celebrates the right to read.

Penguin Random House values and supports copyright. Copyright fuels creativity, encourages
diverse voices, promotes free speech, and creates a vibrant culture. Thank you for buying an
authorized edition of this book and for complying with copyright laws by not reproducing,
scanning, or distributing any part of it in any form without permission. You are supporting
writers and allowing Penguin Random House to continue to publish books for every reader.
Please note that no part of this book may be used or reproduced in any manner for the purpose
of training artificial intelligence technologies or systems.

STEP INTO READING®

SPORTS ARE FUN!

by Zaila Avant-garde
illustrated by Felicia Whaley

Random House 🏠 New York

Sports are fun!

Let's go play!

Be a soccer star.

Kick, kick, score!

Bounce a basketball.

Bounce, bounce, soar!

Run a race.

Huff, puff, run!

I love my team.

Number one!

Flip and fly.

Jump and glide.

Hit it.

Pass it.

Throw it.

Catch it.

Touchdown!

Climbing wall.

Climb!

Bowling pins.

Crash!

Fast skateboard.

Zoom!

Swimming pool.

Splash!

Can you ride?

Can you spin?

Can you swing?

Can you win?

Yes, you can!
Sports are fun!